11

16
115

17

2
16
0
2 3

A Pet's Life

Guinea Pigs

Anita Ganeri

Heinemann
LIBRARY

www.heinemannlibrary.co.uk
Visit our website to find out more information about Heinemann Library books.

To order:
☎ Phone +44 (0) 1865 888066
▤ Fax +44 (0) 1865 314091
▤ Visit www.heinemannlibrary.co.uk

Heinemann Library is an imprint of Capstone Global Library Limited, a company incorporated in England and Wales having its registered office at 7 Pilgrim Street, London, EC4V 6LB – Registered company number: 6695582

"Heinemann" is a registered trademark of Pearson Education Limited, under licence to Capstone Global Library Limited.

Text © Capstone Global Library Limited
Second edition first published in hardback and paperback in 2009.
The moral rights of the proprietor have been asserted.

Edited by Charlotte Guillain and Harriet Milles
Designed by Joanna Hinton-Malivoire
Picture research by Liz Alexander
Production by Victoria Fitzgerald
Originated by Chroma Graphics (Overseas) Pte. Ltd
Printed and bound in China by South China Printing Company Ltd.

ISBN 978 0 4311 7790 8 (hardback)
13 12 11 10 09
10 9 8 7 6 5 4 3 2 1

ISBN 978 0 4311 7797 7 (paperback)
13 12 11 10 09
10 9 8 7 6 5 4 3 2 1

British Library Cataloguing in Publication Data
Ganeri, Anita, 1961-
    Guinea pigs. - 2nd ed. - (A pet's life) (Heinemann first library)
    1. Guinea pigs as pets - Juvenile literature
    I. Title
    636.9'3592
A full catalogue record for this book is available from the British Library.

Acknowledgements
We would like to thank the following for permission to reproduce photographs:
Alamy p. **20** (© Petra Wegner); © Capstone Global Library Ltd pp. **11**, **25**, **27** (Mark Farrell), **4**, **9**, **10**, **12**, **13**, **14**, **15**, **16**, **17**, **18**, **19**, **21**, **23**, **24** (Tudor Photography); Dorling Kindersley p. **6** (Paul Bricknell); RSPCA p. **22** (Angela Hampton); Shutterstock p. **8** (© carsthets); Warren Photographic pp. **5**, **7**, **26** (Jane Burton).

Cover photograph of a guinea pig reproduced with permission of iStockphoto (© Eline Spek).

The publishers would like to thank Rob Lee for his assistance in the preparation of this book.

Every effort has been made to contact copyright holders of material reproduced in this book. Any omissions will be rectified in subsequent printings if notice is given to the publishers.

Contents

Any words appearing in the text in bold, **like this**, are explained in the Glossary.

What do guinea pigs look like?

Guinea pigs are small, furry animals with tiny ears and tails. There are many different kinds and colours of guinea pigs. Some have short fur, and some have long fur.

A guinea pig with short fur, like this one, is best for a first-time pet owner.

This picture shows the different parts of a guinea pig's body. You can see what each part is used for.

Fur. Long-haired guinea pigs need brushing every day to keep their fur free from tangles.

Ears for hearing.

Tiny tail that you can't see!

Beady eyes.

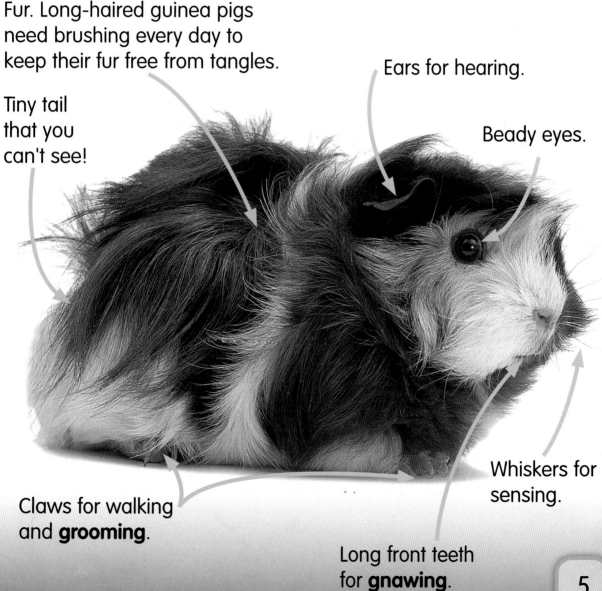

Claws for walking and **grooming**.

Whiskers for sensing.

Long front teeth for **gnawing**.

Guinea pig babies

A mother guinea pig has about four babies in a **litter**. The babies are born with lots of fur and with their eyes open.

The baby guinea pigs drink their mother's milk.

A female guinea pig can have 20 babies a year. So it is best to keep males and females apart.

The babies are old enough to leave their mother when they are about four weeks old. Then they are ready to become pets.

Choosing your guinea pigs

You can buy guinea pigs from good pet shops or guinea pig breeders. **Animal shelters** often need good homes for guinea pigs.

Guinea pigs like company. It is unkind to keep just one as a pet. Choose two males or two females from the same **litter**.

A healthy guinea pig should be lively and alert.

Pick plump guinea pigs with shiny coats. Check that their ears and eyes are clean, and that their teeth are not too long.

Your guinea pigs' house

Your guinea pigs need a large house to live in. It should have a living space with a **wire mesh** front and a sleeping space with a solid door.

Put a layer of wood shavings on the floor, and a good pile of hay for bedding.

For two guinea pigs, the house should measure at least 120 x 60 x 45 cm.

Keep the house outside and raised off the ground. In winter, you can move it inside your home, or into a shed, or garage.

Welcome home

You can bring your guinea pigs home in a small cat-carrying basket or a sturdy box. Leave them for a while so that they can settle into their new home.

Make sure that the carrying box has holes in it so that your guinea pigs can breathe.

Stroke your guinea pig gently and make a fuss of it.

Guinea pigs are quite timid. Be gentle when you pick your pet up. Put one hand under its bottom and the other hand around its shoulders.

Play time

Guinea pigs need lots of space to play and exercise. Make them an outside run in the garden. In cold or wet weather, an indoor **pen** is best.

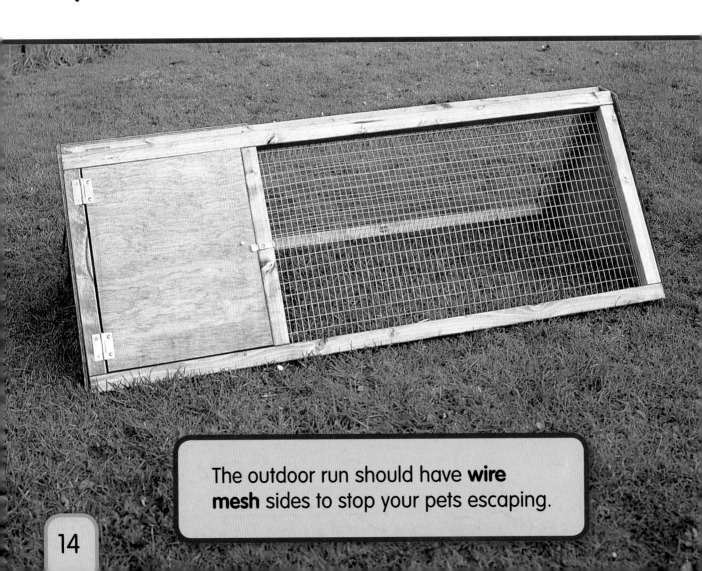

The outdoor run should have **wire mesh** sides to stop your pets escaping.

Don't forget to put some food and water in the run.

Guinea pigs love to play hide and seek. Put some logs, rocks and piles of hay in the run for your pets to explore.

Feeding time

You can buy special guinea pig food from a pet shop. Never feed your guinea pigs rabbit food. Guinea pigs also like to eat chopped fresh fruit and vegetables.

Your guinea pigs need lots of **vitamin C**. They can get this from good hay, greenstuff, raw apples, carrots, and cabbage leaves.

Make sure that your guinea pigs have fresh drinking water every day. Give them a **drip feeder** water bottle.

You should feed your guinea pigs every morning and evening. Put the food in heavy bowls that will not tip over.

Cleaning the house

You can help to keep your guinea pigs healthy by keeping their house clean. Take away any wet bedding, old food, and **droppings** every day.

Put in some fresh wood shavings and lots of hay for bedding.

At least four times a year, give the house a thorough scrub. Leave it to dry before you put your pets back in.

Once a week, empty the house and give it a good clean. You also need to wash out the **drip feeder** water bottle and food bowls. Don't forget to clean the outside run.

Growing up

Guinea pigs grow up quickly. When a male guinea pig is fully grown, it will weigh about the same as a large bag of sugar (1 kg). Female guinea pigs are slightly smaller.

Male guinea pigs are bigger than females.

If your guinea pig whistles, it means that it is hungry, thirsty, or just happy to see you.

Guinea pigs like to talk a lot. They squeak, tweet, chatter, chirrup, and whistle. You will soon get to know what your guinea pig means.

Healthy guinea pigs

Your guinea pigs will stay healthy if you take care of them. If your pets look unwell, take them to a vet straightaway.

If your guinea pig is not eating, seems tired or starts sneezing, it may be ill.

Guinea pigs' front teeth and claws can grow too long. Give your pets a wooden **gnawing** block to wear their teeth down. A vet can trim their claws.

If your guinea pigs' teeth grow too long, they will not be able to eat properly

Your pet guinea pigs

Guinea pigs make wonderful pets and are quite easy to keep. But you must be a good pet owner and care for them properly.

Your guinea pigs will depend on you for all their needs.

Write a list of what your friend should do and leave it by the guinea pigs' house.

Your guinea pigs need food and water every day. If you are going on holiday, ask a friend or neighbour to look after your pets.

Old age

If you look after your guinea pigs, they may live for up to seven years. Guinea pigs hate the cold. You need to make sure they are warm, especially in winter.

As your guinea pig gets older, check it every day to make sure that it is healthy.

It can be very upsetting when your pets die. Try not to be too sad. Just remember the happy times you shared together.

Caring for your guinea pigs will help you learn how to treat animals properly.

Useful tips

- Always wash your hands before and after touching your pets.

- Guinea pigs **groom** themselves. But you need to brush long-haired guinea pigs every day to stop their fur getting tangled. Use a soft toothbrush or a baby's hairbrush.

- If your pet holds its head to one side and cannot walk in a straight line, it may have an ear **infection**. Take it to a vet.

- If your guinea pigs start pulling out each other's fur, it means that they are bored. Make sure that they get plenty of exercise. If your guinea pig is pulling out its own fur, it may have **mange**. Take it to a vet.

- Don't let guinea pigs run around your house. They may chew electric cables.

Fact file

- Wild guinea pigs live in South America.

- Guinea pigs are named after Guiana, the South American country where they were first found.

- Guinea pigs are rodents. They belong to the same group of animals as hamsters, squirrels, mice, and rats.

- Male guinea pigs are called boars and females are called sows, just like real pigs.

- Adult guinea pigs need about 30–50 g of dry food a day, plus 100 g of fresh fruit and vegetables, and lots of hay.

Glossary

animal shelter place where lost or unwanted animals can be looked after

drip feeder bottle that lets water slowly drip out. It is fixed to the guinea pig's house.

droppings guinea pigs' poo

gnaw chew and bite

groom gently brush and clean your guinea pig's fur. Guinea pigs also groom themselves.

infection illness

litter group of baby guinea pigs

mange nasty skin disease

pen large, open box for your guinea pigs to play in indoors

vitamin C goodness from food which guinea pigs need to stay healthy

wire mesh sheet of wire with holes in it

More information

Books to read

Guinea Pigs (First Pets), Laura Howell
(Usborne Publishing Limited, 2005)

Read and Wonder: I Love Guinea Pigs,
Dick King-Smith & Anita Jeram
(Walker Books, 2001)

RSPCA Pet Guide: Care for your Guinea Pig
(Collins, 2004)

Websites

www.rspca.org.uk
The website of The Royal Society for the
Prevention of Cruelty to Animals in Britain.

www.pethealthcare.co.uk
Information about caring for first pets.

www.petlink.com.au
Information about being a good pet owner.

Index